BRAND NEW

BRAND NEW

A 40-DAY GUIDE TO LIFE IN CHRIST

SHILO TAYLOR

LEXHAM PRESS

Brand New: A 40-Day Guide to Life in Christ

Copyright 2017 Shilo Taylor

Lexham Press, 1313 Commercial St., Bellingham, WA 98225
www.LexhamPress.com

Print ISBN 9781683590231
Digital ISBN 9781683590224

Lexham Editorial Team: Todd Hains, Jennifer Stair, and Joel Wilcox
Cover Design: Bryan Hintz
Typesetting: ProjectLuz.com

CONTENTS

PART TWO: THE CHARACTER OF GOD

INTRODUCTION

Welcome to your new beginning. Welcome to playing your part in the greatest story ever. Welcome to the family of faith!

Brand New is a forty-day devotional that will help you establish a foundation for your faith. This short book will answer many of your questions and teach you the basic beliefs of Christianity. You'll learn the story of the Bible: the adventurous love story of God pursuing you. You'll learn who God is and what he is like. You'll learn how to live out your faith.

Our lives aren't meant to be lived alone—and *Brand New* isn't meant to be read alone! As Christians, we all need others to encourage, challenge, and teach us. Although you could read this devotional on your own, you'll get even more out of this book if you read it along with someone who is mature in faith—a mentor, small group leader, pastor, parent, or friend.

Each day of *Brand New* focuses on one aspect of Scripture, God's character, and the Christian life. Each daily devotion includes a key passage from the Bible, an explanation of the topic, a suggested Scripture reading, and reflection questions to help you respond to what God might be showing you.

Discuss the questions and reading with other Christians. Don't be afraid to ask your mentor for help! Grab a blank notebook and journal your thoughts, reflections, and feelings as you read. Memorize or write down the verses that comfort and challenge you.

Each day's devotion closes with prayer. Many of the prayers are paraphrased from the Bible so you can learn how to use God's word in your prayers. Your prayers don't have to sound polished or fancy! The Bible says that the Holy Spirit will help you as you pray. "The Spirit himself intercedes for us through wordless groans" (Romans 8:26). God wants to hear from you! You can pray the written prayers, or you can use your own words to talk with God. Jesus says, "I will do whatever you ask in my name, so that the Father may be glorified in the Son" (John 14:13). So although it's not required to end your prayers with this phrase, each prayer in this devotional ends with "in Jesus' name, amen." (Amen means "so be it.")

Keep *Brand New* on your shelf so you can revisit these daily readings over and over. All Christians continually need to be reminded of the basics of our faith. Something new will stick out to you each time you read through it! Underline, highlight, write notes, and record your thoughts in a notebook or journal. As your faith grows, you'll be encouraged how God has brought you closer to him.

"The LORD bless you and keep you; the LORD make his face shine on you and be gracious to you; the LORD turn his face toward you and give you peace" (Numbers 6:24–26).

Shilo Taylor
Lynden, WA
October 2016

EZEKIEL 36:26-27

I will give you a new heart and put a new spirit in you; I will remove from you your heart of stone and give you a heart of flesh. And I will put my Spirit in you and move you to follow my decrees and be careful to keep my laws.

THE JOURNEY BEGINS

If you declare with your mouth, "Jesus is Lord," and believe in your heart that God raised him from the dead, you will be saved. For it is with your heart that you believe and are justified, and it is with your mouth that you profess your faith and are saved. (Romans 10:9–10)

During a wedding ceremony, two people make a commitment to be together for life. They vow to choose each other every day from that day forward. They leave behind an old life of living for themselves and move forward in a new life together as they are pronounced husband and wife.

It would be ridiculous for the bride and groom to walk back down the aisle, look at each other, and say, "Thanks for the great wedding day, but I'm going to do my own thing now." Or, "That was a great one-day experience, but it does not change me or my life." No! The newlyweds celebrate with a honeymoon to grow closer. They share a home and a life together. Their wedding vows are the starting point of their life together, not the end. They commit to continue to grow in unity.

If you believe Jesus died and rose again to forgive you and to give you true life, if you have asked him to forgive you, if you have asked him to come into your life, then hooray! You have begun an incredible journey with the Lord of the universe. No longer do you have to worry about whether you're good enough for God, because in Christ you are God's own child! Nothing can separate you from the love of God in Christ Jesus. When you feel alone or when you experience guilt and shame, you can turn to God instead of running away from him. You are forgiven!

A relationship with God is better than any other relationship or anything you can buy. It's permanent and will change you more than anything else in your life. Welcome to the beginning of a lifelong journey. (Spoiler alert: this one ends in happily ever after.)

READ

Answer these questions after reading John 3:16–21.

1. What are you excited about in your journey with God?
2. What scares you about your journey with God?
3. According to John 3:17, why did Jesus come to earth?
4. How do Jesus' words in this passage comfort you?

PRAY

Today's prayer comes from John 3:16–21.

> Dear Jesus, I believe you are the Son of God, who came into the world to save those who believe in you. Thank you for coming into my life, forgiving my sins, and having a relationship with me. By your word and Spirit, teach me to grow close to you. Change me as I spend these next forty days learning about you. In your name, amen.

WHAT DOES FREEDOM REALLY MEAN?

You are no longer a slave, but God's child; and since you are his child, God has made you also an heir. (Galatians 4:7)

Have you ever said, "It's my life. I'm free to do whatever makes me happy"? After a while, whatever you choose to pursue—popularity, alcohol, relationships, living selfishly, or trying hard to be perfect—becomes something that controls you instead of you controlling it. Soon the choice doesn't feel like a choice at all. Instead of being free, you're a slave.

Before we commit our lives to Jesus we are slaves to sin. Even if we try to be good, we still aren't free. Freedom is an illusion. We are tangled up in our sin, and it is impossible to set ourselves free. When we commit our lives to Jesus, we are freed from our slavery. Only God brings real freedom. He frees us from everything we've been controlled by. Only God—who is absolutely perfect and all-powerful—can make us his children and save us.

Jesus forgives us. Jesus heals us. Jesus makes us whole. Don't be discouraged if you don't see instant change. The more you know God, the more you will become the person God created you to be. He knows what your purpose is, what is best for you, what you are good at, and how your experiences will be used in the future. He will help you get past what holds you back. He will make you whole.

During the next few weeks we are going to be learning about the story of the Bible, who God is, and how to have a relationship with him.

READ

Answer these questions after reading John 8:31–36.

1. What are some things you have been a "slave" to?
2. Describe what you think it means to be a "slave to sin" (John 8:34).
3. According to verse 32, what will the truth do?
4. How does it feel to know that you are God's child whom he has set free?

PRAY

Today's prayer comes from John 8:31–36.

Heavenly Father, you have set me free from sin. Thank you for revealing the truth of the gospel to me and making me your child. Please teach me what it means to have freedom in you. In Jesus' name, amen.

WHY IS THE BIBLE IMPORTANT?

All Scripture is God-breathed and is useful for teaching, rebuking, correcting and training in righteousness, so that the servant of God may be thoroughly equipped for every good work. (2 Timothy 3:16–17)

Have you ever drawn a line only to find it's not straight? Your freehanded line might look good, but when you put a ruler against it, you discover it's crooked. A ruler helps you realize what's straight and what's not. The Bible is like a ruler for us. Something might look right to us, but when know what the Bible says, we can see that it's actually "crooked."

The Bible is the word of God. We can trust it! It was true when it was written, it is true today, and it will be true forever. The Bible is the standard for Christian faith and action. When we aren't sure if a belief or action is true, we should look at what God says in Scripture. God never contradicts himself. "The word of God is alive and active. Sharper than any double-edged sword, it penetrates even to dividing soul and spirit, joints and marrow; it judges the thoughts and attitudes of the heart" (Hebrews 4:12).

Christians need to know the Bible, to study and memorize it. Psalm 119 calls the Bible a lamp for our feet and a light for our path. In showing us who to follow, it guides who we are and what we do. It builds up. It corrects us. It trains us in the way we should go. God's word is powerful. It's not empty, but instead it accomplishes what God desires.

The Bible teaches the history of God's people and the history of the King and Savior, Jesus Christ. This history is for all believers, even for us today. The Bible shows us who God is and what he has done, still does, and will do. It also shows us who we are and how we should live. Because Christ has already won the victory over sin, death, and the devil, we know that this victory will be ours!

READ

Answer these questions after reading Psalm 1 and 119:105–12.

1. What phrases does the psalmist use to describe God's word?
2. In what ways do you think God's word is like a light that illuminates your path?
3. What Bible verses or passages have you read or heard that encouraged you and brought you joy?
4. Write down a verse that encourages you and post it where you will read it every day (nightstand, mirror, in the car, your phone lock screen).

PRAY

Today's prayer comes from Psalm 119:9-16.

> Lord, your word is pure and true. May I seek you with all my heart, never straying from your commandments. Hide your word in my heart, that I might not sin against you. Blessed are you, O Lord; teach me your decrees! May I declare your word, rejoicing in your statutes as much as in great riches. I will meditate on your precepts and consider your ways. May I delight in your decrees and never neglect your word. In Jesus' name, amen.

THE STORY OF THE BIBLE

GOD'S CREATIVITY FROM THE BEGINNING

*In the beginning God created the heavens and the earth.
Now the earth was formless and empty, darkness was
over the surface of the deep, and the Spirit of God was
hovering over the waters. And God said. ... And it was
so. God saw all that he had made, and it was very good.*
(Genesis 1:1–3, 30–31)

When God created the world, he was pleased with what he
made. It was good. He created something out of nothing,
which is hard for us to understand. God needs nothing and
is truly self-sufficient. Yet he made the earth and everything
in it, demonstrating his power and creativity.

He was particularly excited about the first people he
made, Adam and Eve. "God said, 'Let us make mankind in
our image, in our likeness, so that they may rule over the fish
in the sea and the birds in the sky, over the livestock and all
the wild animals, and over all the creatures that move along
the ground.' So God created mankind in his own image, in

the image of God he created them; male and female he created them. God blessed them." (Genesis 1:26–28).

God created Adam and Eve differently than all the other creatures. He created them in his own image.

Imagine what it was like to be Adam and Eve! No insecurities, achy muscles, or tired brains to slow them down. And God gave them the coolest jobs: naming the animals, exploring the garden, and enjoying his creation with him.

Obeying God was good for Adam and Eve. They were perfect and fulfilled. They weren't lonely or insecure. Every need was met. They lived with purpose in the best relationship with God and with each other. God clearly told them the consequence of disobedience: "You must not eat from the tree of the knowledge of good and evil, for when you eat from it you will certainly die" (Genesis 2:17). Choosing God is choosing life!

READ

Answer these questions after reading Genesis 1–2.

1. What do you think it means to be created in God's image?
2. In what ways does God interact with his creation in these verses?
3. What are some of the specific things that God created?
4. What can we learn about God from observing his creation?

PRAY

Today's prayer comes from Genesis 1:31.

> God, thank you for creating this amazing world and
> everything in it. Help me understand that when you look
> at your creation, *including me,* you say that it is "very
> good." Please give me the strength to obey you every day.
> In Jesus' name, amen.

1 JOHN 1:8-9

If we claim to be without sin, we deceive ourselves and the truth is not in us. If we confess our sins, he is faithful and just and will forgive us our sins and purify us from all unrighteousness.

DAY FIVE

OUR CHOICE

Now the serpent was more crafty than any of the wild animals the LORD God had made. He said to the woman, "Did God really say, 'You must not eat from any tree in the garden'?" (Genesis 3:1)

In Genesis 2:16, God said, "You are free to eat from any tree in the garden; but you must not eat from the tree of the knowledge of good and evil, for when you eat from it you will certainly die." Adam and Eve faced a choice: to obey God, trusting he knows best and has a perfect plan for them, or to do what they want.

The serpent (Satan) knew what to say to get Eve to doubt God. "'You will not certainly die,' the serpent said to the woman. 'For God knows that when you eat from it your eyes will be opened, and you will be like God, knowing good and evil'" (Genesis 3:4–5). She began to wonder if God was holding out on them. Was God as good as they thought? Maybe life would be better if they took things into their own hands. These doubts led to disobedience. "When the woman saw that the fruit of the tree was good for food and pleasing to the eye, and also desirable for gaining wisdom, she took some and ate it. She also gave some to her husband, who was with her, and he ate it" (Genesis 3:6).

When they ate the fruit, Adam and Eve were immediately filled with fear. They realized that by their disobedience they had broken their perfect relationship with God. In place of freedom and openness, they felt shame and guilt. Instead of running to God, who loved them, they tried to run away and hide. Worse yet, when God confronted Adam about eating the fruit, Adam avoided responsibility, blaming God and Eve. "The woman you put here with me—she gave me some fruit from the tree, and I ate it" (Genesis 3:12). Eve, in turn, blamed the serpent.

When we turn away from God as Lord, we sin. God is holy, and he can't tolerate sin. It has to be addressed. Eating fruit doesn't seem like a big deal—*Don't we need to eat? It's only fruit. Should it really change the course of human history?* But their actions revealed that they loved their own lives more than obeying God. Adam and Eve thought they knew better than God. They chose death.

Death, hard work, jealousy, pain, loneliness, and separation from God resulted from their choice. Because of sin we live in a broken world, but it's not supposed to be this way. Everything God made was good. And God has a plan to restore his creation. Before he told Adam and Eve the consequences of their sin, he cursed the serpent and promised future life to Adam and Eve. Adam and Eve wouldn't see the whole plan unfold in their lifetime, but God already had his plan in motion to save his people.

READ

Answer these questions after reading Genesis 3.

1. Have you ever decided that you knew better than God? If so, describe the situation. What were the results?
2. Why did Eve decide to eat the fruit? (See Genesis 3:6.) Do you think looks can be deceiving? Why or why not?
3. Who initiated the relational connection after the sin: Adam and Eve, or God? (See Genesis 3:8–9). Why do you think that is significant?
4. How does Genesis 3:21 show God's love for us?

PRAY

Today's prayer comes from 1 John 1:8–10.

> Heavenly Father, if I claim to be without sin, I deceive myself and the truth is not in me. My thoughts, words, and actions reflect that I often think I know better than you. But if we confess our sins, you are faithful and just to forgive our sins and purify us from all unrighteousness. Please forgive me. I can't fix myself. Thank you for seeking me out and not leaving me in my mess. Help me to trust your plans. In Jesus' name, amen.

THE LIFE IS IN THE BLOOD

The life of a creature is in the blood, and I have given it to you to make atonement for yourselves on the altar; it is the blood that makes atonement for one's life. (Leviticus 17:11)

God loves his people and wants a relationship with them, even after they sinned. But God is holy. He cannot ignore our sin; it must be dealt with. The only suitable consequence for sin is death. But God does not abandon us, even when we abandon him. After Adam and Eve sinned, "The LORD God made garments of skin for Adam and his wife and clothed them" (Genesis 3:21). God killed an innocent animal to cover the guilt, shame, and nakedness of his people. God loves his people and wants a relationship with them.

God later taught his people to make sacrifices. To reestablish a right relationship with God, a person killed an animal as an offering to God. The animal's blood (life) covered the person's sin and shame (death)—just like the animal garments covered Adam and Eve's sin. It symbolized the removal of sin and reconciliation with God.

While his people made animal sacrifices, God had his perfect plan in place. He would someday make a sacrifice that would go beyond all other sacrifices. Instead of animals giving their lifeblood to make us right with God, he would send his Son to shed his blood and give his life as the final, perfect sacrifice. Jesus is "the Lamb of God, who takes away the sin of the world" (John 1:29). All Old Testament sacrifices point to Jesus.

God's plan to send his Son would not only temporarily *cover* sin, but Jesus' death and resurrection would *remove* sin. Forever. Jesus is the only truly innocent and perfect sacrifice. Only through his death and resurrection are we made whole. Jesus forgives us and brings us peace, joy, and true life.

READ

Answer these questions after reading Leviticus 9:1–24 and Hebrews 9.

1. What are some things you have done
   to try to earn God's love? Why?
2. How do you handle guilt and shame?
3. Why do you think God commanded the Israelites
   to offer animal sacrifices? (See Hebrews 9:22–23.)
4. In what ways was Christ's sacrifice of himself
   better than the animal sacrifices?

PRAY

Today's prayer comes from Psalm 51:7–12.

Lord, cleanse me and I will be clean; wash me and I will be whiter than snow. Let me hear joy and gladness; let me rejoice in you. Hide your face from my sins and blot out my iniquity. Create in me a pure heart, O God, and renew a steadfast spirit within me. Do not cast me from your presence or take your Holy Spirit from me. Restore to me the joy of your salvation and grant me a willing spirit, to sustain me. In Jesus' name, amen.

THE NIGHT THE LORD PASSED OVER

The blood will be a sign for you on the houses where you are, and when I see the blood, I will pass over you. No destructive plague will touch you when I strike Egypt. (Exodus 12:13)

The Israelites spent 430 years as slaves in Egypt. (Genesis 37–50 tells how they got there.) Pharaoh was determined to keep the Israelites as slaves, but God had promised to rescue them and bring them to the promised land (you can read this promise in Genesis 15:18). He struck Egypt with nine plagues, but Pharaoh still refused to obey and let the Israelites go. Ultimately God will do what he says he will do. He was determined to rescue his people.

The last plague was the death of the firstborn, recorded in Exodus 12. The Israelites were instructed to sacrifice a perfect, spotless lamb. Each family smeared the blood of that lamb on the doorpost of their home to show that a lamb had died in place of the oldest son. The sacrificed lamb showed they were God's protected children, and the Lord passed over their home. They were spared from judgment and death. Then, they cooked the lamb's meat to give them strength—they were about to flee Egypt and would need it for the journey ahead! The Israelites celebrated this night of judgment and mercy as a yearly feast called Passover.

God is the holy and supreme Judge, who punishes sin. At the same time, he is our Rescuer, who loves us. Passover points to Jesus. Anyone who believes in Jesus is God's own. "We have been made holy through the sacrifice of the body of Jesus Christ once for all" (Hebrews 10:10). Jesus covered the doorposts of our soul with his own blood to save us from judgment.

READ

Answer these questions after reading Exodus 12.

1. What do God's actions in Exodus 12 tell you about his character?
2. How does this passage reveal both God's justice (v. 12) and also his mercy (v. 13)?
3. Based on what you read in Exodus 12, why do you think John the Baptist calls Jesus "the Lamb of God" (John 1:29)?
4. What is Jesus called in 1 Corinthians 5:7? Why is that significant?

PRAY

Today's prayer comes from Deuteronomy 7:8-9.

> Lord, we were slaves to sin, but you have rescued us with your mighty hand. You redeemed us with the blood of Christ. Thank you for calling us to be your people. Remind us that we are free in Christ and don't have to live like slaves to sin. In Jesus' name, amen.

THE LAW AND THE WILDERNESS WALK

Moses went up to God, and the LORD called to him from the mountain and said, "This is what you are to say to the descendants of Jacob and what you are to tell the people of Israel: 'You yourselves have seen what I did to Egypt, and how I carried you on eagles' wings and brought you to myself. Now if you obey me fully and keep my covenant, then out of all nations you will be my treasured possession. Although the whole earth is mine, you will be for me a kingdom of priests and a holy nation.'" (Exodus 19:3–6)

God chose the Israelites to be his special people. He gave them the Ten Commandments to reveal his perfect character. He demanded that, as his people, the Israelites live in a way that reflected his holiness. "I am the LORD your God; consecrate yourselves and be holy, because I am holy" (Leviticus 11:44). The Israelites couldn't keep these commandments—and neither can we. Even when people fail, God is faithful. He wants a relationship with us. "I will walk among you and be your God, and you will be my people" (Leviticus 26:12).

The Israelites learned that God is their powerful provider. They fled Egypt after the tenth plague. God led them by pillar of fire at night and a pillar of cloud by day. He parted the Red Sea for the Israelites but drowned the pursuing Egyptian soldiers. The Lord made undrinkable water drinkable and provided water out of a rock. He provided bread from heaven every single day. Again and again God showed his faithfulness. Again and again he provided the impossible.

Yet the Israelites doubted God's power and provision when they saw the people who were living in the promised land. They panicked, thinking they couldn't defeat these mighty people—and they didn't believe God would equip them to defeat these enemies and take possession of the land he had promised to them. Because of their unbelief they wandered for the next forty years in the desert.

The Israelites spent those forty years learning they couldn't do life without God. They tried making idols, fighting their own enemies, and solving their own problems only to fall flat on their faces. They learned to repent of their sin—to be truly sad and turn away from it. They learned that obedience leads to blessing and that the presence of God is *everything*. They learned to pray, worship, care for one another, to be warriors, and to hear the voice of God.

At times you might feel like you are wandering in the wilderness. Remember that God is always powerful and in control. He will use your journey—like the Israelites' journey thousands of years ago—to draw you closer to himself and to show you his faithfulness. "The LORD your God has blessed you in all the work of your hands. He has watched over your journey through this vast wilderness. These forty years the LORD your God has been with you, and you have not lacked anything" (Deuteronomy 2:7).

READ

Answer these questions after reading Exodus 20.

1. Why would God's presence have been frightening to the Israelites?
2. Do you think God's presence is frightening now? Why or why not?
3. In what ways are the Ten Commandments good for us?
4. What do the Ten Commandments reveal to us about God's character?

PRAY

Today's prayer comes from Exodus 20.

> You are the Lord our God, who delivers us from the slavery of our sin. Teach me to worship you, to honor

your name, to hear your word diligently, and to obey you. Thank you for creating and redeeming me. In Jesus' name, amen.

LEVITICUS 26:12

I will walk among you and be your God, and you will be my people.

DAY NINE

THE PLAN FORETOLD

He was pierced for our transgressions, he was crushed for our iniquities; the punishment that brought us peace was on him, and by his wounds we are healed. We all, like sheep, have gone astray, each of us has turned to our own way; and the LORD has laid on him the iniquity of us all. (Isaiah 53:5–6)

Written more than five hundred years before Jesus' birth, these verses in the Old Testament describe Jesus' death on the cross for the forgiveness of sin. God gave these words to the prophet Isaiah. Prophets were people who proclaimed and interpreted God's word. Sometimes they explained God's promises. Sometimes they explained God's judgment. Sometimes they described future events. In fact, the psalmist and the prophet Zechariah described that Jesus' hands and feet would be pierced, even before crucifixion was invented! These prophecies had a fuller meaning than what the prophets themselves may have understood.

God had a plan to save us before the creation of the world. Sending his Son was not a spur-of-the-moment decision. God knew what would happen from the beginning. Although we all have turned our backs on God and sinned against him, God took our suffering on himself and became our sacrifice. Jesus is the Suffering Servant. He willingly went to the cross to die for us. Instead of complaining or leaving us in our own helplessness, he allowed himself to be pierced and killed for our sin. He rose from the dead and shared his victory over sin and death with us. Because of him we have a new, restored relationship with God!

These prophecies excited God's people. They knew something big was going to happen, and it would bring them freedom. They knew it would give them a closer relationship with God. They didn't know exactly how or when it would happen, but they believed God would keep his promise.

READ

Answer these questions after reading Isaiah 52:13–53:12.

1. What does it mean that all our sins were laid on Jesus? (See Isaiah 53:6.)
2. In what ways can you identify with the statement: "We all, like sheep, have gone astray" (Isaiah 53:6)?
3. How does this passage help you understand your sin and Jesus' sacrifice?
4. What are some of the results of Jesus' death, according to Isaiah 53:10–12?

PRAY

Today's prayer comes from Isaiah 53:5-6.

> Jesus, you were pierced for our transgressions and crushed for our iniquities. You took the sin of us all and paid our penalty on the cross. Thank you for always having the perfect plan for us. Thank you for offering me relationship with you because of your sacrifice. Help me understand your word and apply it to my life. In your name, amen.

THE PLAN UNFOLDS

So Joseph also went up from the town of Nazareth in Galilee to Judea, to Bethlehem the town of David, because he belonged to the house and line of David. He went there to register with Mary, who was pledged to be married to him and was expecting a child. While they were there, the time came for the baby to be born, and she gave birth to her firstborn, a son. She wrapped him in cloths and placed him in a manger, because there was no guest room available for them. (Luke 2:4–7)

For centuries, the Israelites had read the prophecies about God coming to free them. Many had memorized these passages and were eagerly waiting for the Messiah. But many expected a glamorous and mighty king who would conquer their oppressors and bring political freedom. As a result they expected that, as God's people, they would gain respect and power. They thought the Messiah would act like other powerful earthly kings.

But God's plan was different. God came to earth as a defenseless baby in a smelly barn. His parents were humble, ordinary, faithful people. Angels declared his birth to grubby shepherds and foreign wise men, not to politicians or religious leaders.

Jesus didn't come to add rules, hang out with religious people, or act like a normal king. He came to fulfill God's law, hang out with sinners, and die and rise again to cover our sin with his righteousness and forgiveness. He came to help people who desperately needed his help. He came for the hurting, the fearful, the guilty. He came to make us whole, to teach us, to comfort us, and to make us his. He came for you and me! By his wounds he heals us. By his death he gives us life. By his word and Spirit he transforms us to become like him.

READ

Answer these questions after reading Luke 1–2.

1. What were the circumstances surrounding Jesus' birth? If you were God, looking for a place for your own Son to be born on earth, would you have chosen this situation? Why or why not?
2. What do you think the shepherds thought when they saw the angels? How does their response to the angel's announcement serve as an example for us?

3. What would you have thought about
   Jesus if you saw him as a baby?
4. What did you learn in these verses about God's plan?

PRAY

Today's prayer comes from Luke 1:38 and 2:31.

> Father, nothing is impossible with you! Thank you for
> sending Jesus, who is your salvation, which you have
> prepared in the sight of all nations. I am your servant;
> may your word to me be fulfilled. Please transform me
> to be more like Jesus every day. In Jesus' name, amen.

REPENT, FOR THE KINGDOM OF HEAVEN HAS COME NEAR

In those days John the Baptist came, preaching in the wilderness of Judea and saying, "Repent, for the kingdom of heaven has come near." This is he who was spoken of through the prophet Isaiah: "A voice of one calling in the wilderness, 'Prepare the way for the Lord, make straight paths for him.'" (Matthew 3:1-3)

God gave John the Baptist an important job: to prepare people for Jesus. John's message was simple. He didn't hand out checklists telling people, "Straighten out your life! Jesus is coming!" He knew Jesus was going to do something much deeper than make people look religious and moral. He wanted to address the condition of their heart, not their actions. To prepare for Jesus, repentance comes first.

Repentance is an action, not a fickle feeling. It's not just apologizing, feeling guilty, or being sorry for getting caught.

Repentance is turning away from our wrong thoughts and actions and turning toward Jesus. When we repent we are deeply sad over our sin and the hurt it has caused. We are grieved that our sin breaks our relationship with God. We apologize and ask for forgiveness. It doesn't mean we suddenly become perfect. We understand we can't make things right or fix it without Jesus. We need to ask Jesus to help us change our hearts and our behavior by his Spirit.

John taught we can't just do our best to be good Christians or try to clean up our life before we ask God into it. We can't jump into doing good things for Jesus and skip repentance. The religious people in Jesus' day wanted a gold star for their good deeds, but Jesus turned everything upside down. "It is not the healthy who need a doctor, but the sick," he said. "I have not come to call the righteous, but sinners" (Mark 2:17). Our relationship with Jesus starts with acknowledging that we need him. Apart from Christ, we can't honor God or be in right relationship with him. We ask him to forgive our sins and to make us like him.

READ

Answer these questions after reading 2 Corinthians 7:2–16.

1. How would you define *repentance*?
2. What do you need to repent of? In what areas do you need God's strength to help you change?

3. Have you ever experienced "godly sorrow" over a sin? If so, describe the situation.
4. According to 2 Corinthians 7:10, what is the result of repentance?

PRAY

Today's prayer comes from Psalm 25:5–8, 11, 20–21.

Lord, guide me in your truth and teach me, for you are God my Savior. Remember your great mercy and love, not the sins of my youth and my rebellious ways. According to your love remember me, for you, O Lord, are good. Because you are good and upright, you instruct sinners in your ways. For the sake of your name, Lord, forgive my sin, though it is great. Guard my life and rescue me; do not let me be put to shame, for I take refuge in you. May integrity and uprightness protect me, because my hope, Lord, is in you! In Jesus' name, amen.

JESUS IS ONE PERSON, FULLY GOD AND FULLY HUMAN

In your relationships with one another, have the same mindset as Christ Jesus: Who, being in very nature God, did not consider equality with God something to be used to his own advantage; rather, he made himself nothing by taking the very nature of a servant, being made in human likeness. And being found in appearance as a man, he humbled himself by becoming obedient to death— even death on a cross! (Philippians 2:5–8)

Jesus is fully God and fully human. The Bible teaches that Jesus is both God's Son and also Mary's son. The One through whom all things were created was born as a baby. He who sustains the world was sustained by his mother's milk. He satisfies our every need, yet he experienced hunger and thirst. He who alone grants growth grew. Jesus, who comforts us, experienced pain in every way—emotionally, physically, and spiritually. We pray to him and he prayed to our Father in heaven. He has always been and always will be!

Remember that the animal chosen for sacrifice in the Old Testament had to be without blemish, perfect, the best of the flock? That sacrifice points to Jesus, who was the perfect sacrifice for us. We weren't bought with cash. We were purchased out of our empty, sin-filled life by Jesus Christ's own blood to live a full, grace-filled life.

Only Jesus, who is fully God and fully human, could be this perfect sacrifice. In order to be an effective mediator between us and God, Jesus had to be human so that he could identify with us and sinless so that he could die to pay the penalty for our sins (and not need a mediator for his own sins). The mediator had to keep the law perfectly. Only God is perfect. So the mediator could only be God! The mediator also had to be able to share our nature, so that we can share in his victory. So God became man for us. Jesus, true God and true man, reconciled sinners to the one holy God— by dying and rising again. He came as a humble baby, and he conquered sin, death, and the devil!

READ

Answer these questions after reading Hebrews 4:14–5:10.

1. In what ways is Jesus able to empathize with us?
2. Why can we approach the throne of grace more confidently when we know that Jesus can empathize with us?

3. How should it affect your daily frustrations and joys to know that Jesus experienced everything you are facing—sin, doubt, fear, joy?

4. What do you learn about Jesus' prayer life in Hebrews 5:7?

PRAY

Today's prayer comes from the Apostles' Creed, the historic declaration of faith.

I believe in Jesus Christ, his only Son, our Lord. He was conceived by the Holy Spirit and born of the Virgin Mary. He suffered under Pontius Pilate, was crucified, died, and was buried. He descended to the dead. On the third day he rose again from the dead. He ascended into heaven. He is seated at the right hand of the Father. He will come to judge the living and the dead. In Jesus' name, amen.

JOHN 14:6

I am the way and the truth and the life. No one comes to the Father except through me.

DAY THIRTEEN

JESUS' MINISTRY ON EARTH

Jesus went throughout Galilee, teaching in their syna-gogues, proclaiming the good news of the kingdom, and healing every disease and sickness among the people. News about him spread all over Syria, and people brought to him all who were ill with various diseases, those suffering severe pain, the demon-possessed, those having seizures, and the paralyzed; and he healed them. Large crowds from Galilee, the Decapolis, Jerusalem, Judea and the region across the Jordan followed him. (Matthew 4:23–25)

Jesus came to earth with great purpose: to proclaim the kingdom of God, to die, and to rise again. By his death and resurrection, he defeated death, forgiving our sin and grant-ing us true life. His life, death, resurrection, and ascension are gifts for us, and they're also examples to us. Jesus shows us how to love God and others.

Jesus' earthly ministry kicked off with his baptism in the Jordan River. It was an incredible sight. As Jesus came out of the water the Holy Spirit came down like a dove and God's voice could be heard saying, "This is my Son, whom I love; with him I am well pleased" (Matthew 3:17). After his baptism, Jesus spent forty days in the wilderness, praying and preparing for what was to come. During those forty days Satan tempted Jesus to try to get him to use his power for his own worldly benefit instead of staying in line with God's plan. However, Jesus resisted Satan with Scripture and won, standing firm against temptation.

When Jesus returned from the wilderness, he preached the kingdom of God, cast out demons, and performed miracles. His message was simple: "The kingdom of God has come near. Repent and believe the good news!" (Mark 1:15). Jesus chose twelve disciples, sending them out to proclaim the kingdom and perform miracles. He also taught them about God's blessing, the law, prayer, judgment, and truth.

During his ministry on earth, Jesus rooted his actions in his message of love and forgiveness. His actions and his message stopped people in their tracks. With power and authority Jesus commanded demons to flee, wind and weather to be calm, the sick to be well, the crippled to walk, the blind to see, the deaf to hear, the mute to speak, and the dead to rise.

Jesus' message and might made the political and religious leaders uncomfortable and suspicious of him. He was a threat to their power! Worse yet, he openly confronted their abuse and oppression. He spoke against their hypocrisy and stopped them from ripping people off in the temple, reestablishing it as a place of worship. Jesus knew that his words and deeds would upset the political and religious leaders who were in power. He warned his followers that he would die, but that they should not fear because he would rise from the dead.

Jesus' miracles and message are the same today. We believe in him, knowing that he is in control even when our circumstances look different than we expect.

READ

Answer these questions after reading Matthew 4:1-11; Mark 2:1-12; Mark 7; Mark 8.

1. How does it help you to know Jesus was tempted too?
2. How does Jesus use Scripture? In what ways could you apply that practice in your own life?
3. Why do you think the powerful political and religious leaders felt threatened by Jesus?
4. Over what and whom does Jesus have power?

PRAY

Thank God for something you learned about Jesus' life today.

Today's prayer comes from John 17:3-4, 13-19.

Father, eternal life is to know you and Jesus Christ.
May we bring you glory by doing your will. Teach us
to do your will. Give us your joy. Protect us from evil.
Make us more like you as your word changes us. In Jesus'
name, amen.

JESUS' DEATH ON THE CROSS

The governor's soldiers took Jesus into the Praetorium and gathered the whole company of soldiers around him. They stripped him and put a scarlet robe on him, and then twisted together a crown of thorns and set it on his head. They put a staff in his right hand. Then they knelt in front of him and mocked him. "Hail, king of the Jews!" they said. They spit on him, and took the staff and struck him on the head again and again. After they had mocked him, they took off the robe and put his own clothes on him. Then they led him away to crucify him. (Matthew 27:27–31)

Jesus died in a way reserved for the worst criminals: on a cross. Crucifixion was a humiliating, ugly, horrific, public way to die.

Jesus was betrayed by his closest disciples. One of them turned Jesus into the chief priests for thirty pieces of silver.

Another denied knowing Jesus at all when things began to heat up. Jesus was falsely found guilty at an unfair trial. He was beaten severely. People mocked and taunted him, insisting he was powerless. The crowds demanded his death, shouting, "Crucify him" and, "His blood is on us and our children" (Matthew 27:22, 25). He was executed between two criminals on a cross for everyone to see.

Three times Jesus warned his followers about his coming death and resurrection. But they didn't understand. They seemed to think that Jesus' kingdom would be like other earthly kingdoms—thrones, armies, vanquished nations, and plunder. They responded to Jesus' warnings with disbelief, grief, and a desire for power. They dismissed his words, because they were convinced their own idea of victory would transpire. Contrary to their expectations of worldly glory, Jesus died a terrible death. The disciples questioned everything Jesus had said and done. They fled, fearing for their own lives.

Jesus suffered for us on the cross. He set aside comfort and earthly dominance to be the perfect sacrifice. He wasn't interested in the temporary but in our eternity with him. His death was a gift: he bore our sins to heal us. His death was also an example for us: despite insults and false accusations, Jesus didn't retaliate. Instead he entrusted himself to the one just Judge, his Father. By his death Jesus broke the power of death and the devil, freeing us for true life with God.

And the story doesn't end with Jesus' death! "After he has suffered, he will see the light of life and be satisfied" (Isaiah 53:11).

READ

Answer these questions after reading Matthew 26–27.

1. Why do you think Peter struggled to accept God's plan?
2. According to Matthew 26:56, how did Jesus' disciples respond to his arrest?
3. What impacted you most today as you read about Jesus' crucifixion in Matthew 27?
4. What convinced the guards that Jesus was the Son of God in Matthew 27:54?

PRAY

Today's prayer comes from 1 Peter 2:21–25.

Jesus, you suffered for us, giving us a gift and example. You entrusted yourself to the Father. You bore our sins in your body on the cross, so that we might die to sin and live for righteousness. By your wounds we have been healed. Strengthen and guide your people. In your name, amen.

JESUS' RESURRECTION

After the Sabbath, at dawn on the first day of the week, Mary Magdalene and the other Mary went to look at the tomb. ... The angel said to the women, "Do not be afraid, for I know that you are looking for Jesus, who was crucified. He is not here; he has risen, just as he said. Come and see the place where he lay. Then go quickly and tell his disciples: 'He has risen from the dead and is going ahead of you into Galilee. There you will see him.' Now I have told you." So the women hurried away from the tomb, afraid yet filled with joy, and ran to tell his disciples. Suddenly Jesus met them. "Greetings," he said. They came to him, clasped his feet and worshiped him. (Matthew 28:1–9)

After Jesus' death his followers were shocked and scared. Grief and fear turned the disciples' lives upside down. Many were terrified; they gathered secretly behind locked doors, fearing they would be executed next. Many were disappointed, saying, "We had hoped that he was the one who was going to redeem Israel" (Luke 24:21). Some even returned to their old way of life, as if Jesus' life and ministry had never happened. They were grieving and trying to make sense of all that had happened.

On the third day Jesus rose from the dead. He sought out his grieving and disillusioned followers to encourage and comfort them. He shared his peace with them and told them not to fear. Again he patiently showed them how Scripture explained his death and resurrection. This time they were able to listen to him. He sent them to make disciples, to proclaim the good news that death and sin had been defeated in him, and to obey his commands.

Death has no power over God. When Jesus rose from the dead, he revealed the victory he had won over death. God and Satan are not equal. Good and evil are not equal. Jesus was not crucified because people were more powerful than he was, but because he chose to die to be a sacrifice for us. Even when death looked to be winning, God's plan for salvation was still ahead. The nightmare had ended. Jesus is alive! He was right all along.

"Death has been swallowed up in victory. Where, O death, is your victory? Where, O death, is your sting?" (1 Corinthians 15:54–55).

READ

Answer these questions after reading John 20.

1. According to John 20:19–20, how did the disciples feel before they saw the resurrected Jesus? How did they feel after they saw Jesus?
2. How do Jesus' words in John 20:29 encourage you?
3. Why is Jesus' resurrection important? What did Jesus accomplish by rising from the dead?
4. If you believe Jesus died and rose again, how should that impact your life? How should it impact your decisions and actions?

PRAY

Today's prayer comes from 1 Corinthians 15:55–57.

Dear Jesus, you are my victorious Lord! You won the victory over sin and took away the sting of death. Thank you for becoming human, dying, and rising again to forgive my sins and give me true life. Thank you for understanding and identifying with me. Teach me to grow in your love, peace, and joy. In your name, amen.

JESUS' ASCENSION

He was taken up before their very eyes, and a cloud hid him from their sight. They were looking intently up into the sky as he was going, when suddenly two men dressed in white stood beside them. "Men of Galilee," they said, "why do you stand here looking into the sky? This same Jesus, who has been taken from you into heaven, will come back in the same way you have seen him go into heaven." (Acts 1:9–11)

In another surprising twist for the disciples, Jesus didn't stick around on earth indefinitely. But he didn't leave his followers hanging, either! Jesus promised that the Holy Spirit would come and dwell in believers, giving them God's power throughout their lives.

After assuring his followers that they would be equipped for the work he was giving them, Jesus ascended to heaven. He took his place at the right hand of God as King. Because Jesus ascended into heaven, we have the sure promise that we also belong to the kingdom of heaven. Right now we reign with Christ spiritually, but one day we will reign with him and dwell with him fully! God's kingdom is the only kingdom that is not temporary. No other kingdom or power rivals Christ's. And we reign with Christ!

As co-heirs of Jesus' power, we are called to tell others about Jesus' suffering, his resurrection, and the forgiveness of sin in his name. This kingdom isn't up in the sky—"why do you stand here looking into the sky?" (Acts 1:11)—it's here now among believers by the Holy Spirit. "And God placed all things under his feet and appointed him to be head over everything for the church, which is his body, the fullness of him who fills everything in every way" (Ephesians 1:22-23).

Through faith in Jesus we have received the power and majesty of his kingdom. Let's live like it! "The holy people of the Most High will receive the kingdom and will possess it forever—yes, for ever and ever" (Daniel 7:18).

READ

Answer these questions after reading Luke 24:44-53.

1. Have you ever been confused by a passage of Scripture that you couldn't understand? If so, how do Jesus' words in Luke 24:45 encourage you?
2. According to Jesus, what do the Scriptures say about the Messiah?
3. What was Jesus doing when he ascended into heaven?
4. How did the disciples respond when they watched Jesus be taken up into heaven?

PRAY

Today's prayer comes from Psalm 47:5-9

> King Jesus, you have ascended with shouts of joy! You
> reign over the nations. Teach us to sing your praises, for
> you are the King of all the heavens and earth. By your
> word and Spirit rule our hearts and minds, so that we
> might ascend and dwell with you forever and ever. In
> your name, amen.

ISAIAH 41:10

So do not fear, for I am with you;
do not be dismayed, for I am
your God. I will strengthen you
and help you; I will uphold you
with my righteous right hand.

PENTECOST AND LIVING IN THE IN-BETWEEN

In the last days, God says, I will pour out my Spirit on all people. Your sons and daughters will prophesy, your young men will see visions, your old men will dream dreams. Even on my servants, both men and women, I will pour out my Spirit in those days, and they will prophesy. (Acts 2:17–18)

Jesus promised his continued presence with his people. The Holy Spirit is this presence. The Holy Spirit gave them wisdom and courage to tell the world about Jesus. They needed courage—most of them bailed on Jesus when he went to the cross. They were terrified and confused, but that was about to change. "You will receive power when the Holy Spirit comes on you; and you will be my witnesses in Jerusalem, and in all Judea and Samaria, and to the ends of the earth" (Acts 1:8). The Holy Spirit wasn't just for the first disciples; he is with believers today! The Holy Spirit gives us truth, courage, and power, so that we can minister to the world. He dwells in us and draws us to God.

The book of Acts narrates the start of the church after Jesus ascended to heaven. The early Christians preached the gospel in power and without fear, adding thousands to the church. They healed the sick and made cripples walk. They cast out demons. They brought the dead to life. They also suffered persecution—even to the point of death—and division. In all this the Holy Spirit ministered to, strengthened, and equipped the followers of Jesus.

Jesus has defeated death and sin through dying and rising again; however, he hasn't yet returned to judge the world and make everything right and perfect again. We live in this in-between time. We still sin and struggle, but we also have forgiveness and the hope that it won't be like this forever! He has given us his Holy Spirit for power, wisdom, and courage.

He has also given us a mission: to tell the world the good news that he forgives and leads us when we believe and trust him! The New Testament is filled with stories of the church and how Jesus' followers live in this in-between, and it reminds us that we are living for something bigger than just ourselves.

"The Lord is the Spirit, and where the Spirit of the Lord is, there is freedom. And we all, who with unveiled faces contemplate the Lord's glory, are being transformed into

his image with ever-increasing glory, which comes from the
Lord, who is the Spirit" (2 Corinthians 3:17–18).

READ

Answer these questions after reading Acts 2.

1. How did the disciples respond to being called
   drunkards, liars, and crazy people?
2. How do you tend to respond to people
   who don't agree with you?
3. What are some of the things that the
   early church did? (See Acts 2:42–47.)
4. According to Acts 2:47, how did God respond
   to the early church's faithful obedience?

PRAY

Today's prayer comes from Psalm 16:8–11.

Lord, you are always before me. Because you are at my
right hand, I will not be shaken. My heart is glad and my
tongue rejoices; my body will rest secure, because you
will not abandon me to realm of the dead. Jesus did not
decay but rose again, giving us freedom and life. By the
power of the Holy Spirit, make known to me the path
of life and fill me with joy in your presence. In Jesus'
name, amen.

JESUS IS COMING BACK

Then will appear the sign of the Son of Man in heaven. And then all the peoples of the earth will mourn when they see the Son of Man coming on the clouds of heaven, with power and great glory. And he will send his angels with a loud trumpet call, and they will gather his elect from the four winds, from one end of the heavens to the other. (Matthew 24:30–31)

Jesus promised to come again. Once again, the disciples had their own idea of what Jesus meant. They expected to see him return to earth in their lifetime. When it didn't happen the way they expected, some began to doubt whether Jesus would ever return. However, Jesus never said when he would return—in fact, he said no one but God the Father knows the hour. Instead, he told us to always expect his return, so that we would be prepared. "Therefore keep watch, because you do not know on what day your Lord will come. ... You also must be ready, because the Son of

Man will come at an hour when you do not expect him" (Matthew 24:42, 44).

God never forgets his people! His timing is intentional. God delays Jesus' return, because he is merciful. "The Lord is not slow in keeping his promise, as some understand slowness. Instead he is patient with you, not wanting anyone to perish, but everyone to come to repentance" (2 Peter 3:9). God wants everyone to turn to him, and he gives plenty of time and opportunity.

Jesus said he will come again, so he will! Jesus' second coming will bring an end to sin, sickness, and sadness. It will be the ultimate, forever victory. He wants us to be ready. He wants us to be intentional about the time he gives us here on earth. We aren't here to chase things that give only temporary happiness. He has given us a meaningful purpose: to know him, to follow him in obedience, and to share his love with others. "You ought to live holy and godly lives as you look forward to the day of God and speed its coming" (2 Peter 3:11–12).

God has a plan, and we're part of it, so let's be faithful!

READ

Answer these questions after reading Matthew 24.

1. Why is it important to know the Bible and God's promises? (See Matthew 24:3–13.)
2. Why shouldn't you be afraid of things to come? (See Matthew 24:35.)

3. Based on Matthew 24:36, how should you respond when you hear about someone who has predicted a specific date for the end of the world?
4. How seriously do you take the job Jesus has given you to "keep watch" (Matthew 24:42)?

PRAY

Today's prayer comes from John 14:1–3.

Heavenly Father, some things in the world distract me from you; they make me afraid and unsure about the future. But you are certain and your victory is certain. You have promised that you are preparing a place for me in heaven, and you will return to take me to be with you. Please give me peace and faith in your plan and give me courage to tell others about you. In Jesus' name, amen.

HEAVEN

"He will wipe every tear from their eyes. There will be no more death or mourning or crying or pain, for the old order of things has passed away." He who was seated on the throne said, "I am making everything new!" Then he said, "Write this down, for these words are trustworthy and true." (Revelation 21:4–5)

The God who created heaven is the same God who created mountains for us to climb and ski, and oceans for us to surf and snorkel. He created us to love, to be skillful, to learn, to be curious, to enjoy relationship with each other and with him. He made us creative, adventurous, and unique.

Our God has prepared a heaven better than earth in every single way. Every hope and expectation will be surpassed. Imagine the best things on earth: favorite smells, tastes, sights, hobbies, and places. Those are merely shadows of what heaven will be. Your dream job, your closest relationships, your ideal home—all of it pales compared to what God has in store for us!

If your idea of heaven is floating on a cloud, playing a harp, and sitting around twiddling your thumbs for eternity, then get that idea out of your head. We will have a perfect relationship with God and one another. We won't have anything to hide or be embarrassed about. We won't be left out. We will do what we love as worship to God. Our lives and jobs will be meaningful. We won't be less of what God created us to be here on earth, we will be more ourselves than we can ever be on earth.

READ

Answer these questions after reading Revelation 21–22

1. What images and ideas do you think about when you picture heaven?
2. How has your idea of heaven changed after reading today's Bible verses?
3. What are some of the things that will not be in heaven? (See Revelation 21:4.)
4. What excites you about heaven?

PRAY

Today's prayer comes from John 14:1–4.

Dear Lord, you have prepared a place for us. I confess that I can get wrapped up in my life and what's going on here on earth. Please help me focus my heart and mind on you. Teach me to trust and to hope in you. May my anticipation of heaven impact the way I live my life for you today! Come, Lord Jesus. In your name, amen.

THE CHARACTER
OF GOD

GOD IS A MYSTERY

*Great is the LORD and most worthy of praise; his greatness
no one can fathom.* (Psalm 145:3)

My elderly grandmother has studied the Bible her whole
life. One evening as my grandfather read a chapter, I noticed
that her lips moved along with my grandfather's reading.
She knew every word; still, she focused as though she was
hearing it for the first time. She told me afterward, "In
every season of my life I have understood those words and
God differently. It will never get old because he is so much
more than I could ever discover." Even though she has read
through the Bible dozens of times and known Jesus for more
than 80 years, she's still learning. By his word and Spirit,
God continually speaks to her current circumstances.

Knowing the entire Bible doesn't mean you have God
all figured out. You might know all the answers at Bible
study, and you might know Bible characters such as Noah,
Jonah, and the disciples forward, backward, and upside
down. Yet God wants to reveal more to you! He wants to

speak into your life. As you get to know God, the surprises will keep coming. He is deeper, more incomprehensible, and more multidimensional than you will ever know. You will always have more to discover about God in your relationship with him.

We won't ever have all of our questions answered about God. No one person has all the right answers. We are made in God's image. But we are limited; God is limitless, vast, and deeper than anything we can comprehend. "'For my thoughts are not your thoughts, neither are your ways my ways,' declares the LORD. 'As the heavens are higher than the earth, so are my ways higher than your ways and my thoughts than your thoughts'" (Isaiah 55:8–9).

Our human minds will never get it all, but as we seek him through the Bible and prayer, he will grow our understanding. "Call to me and I will answer you and tell you great and unsearchable things you do not know" (Jeremiah 33:3).

READ

Answer these questions after reading Romans 11:33–36.

1. What did you learn about about God's wisdom?
2. Why do you think that no matter how much we learn about God, there is always more of God for us to know?
3. How are you encouraged to know your relationship with God will continue to grow?
4. What new things have you learned about God in the last couple of weeks?

PRAY

Today's prayer comes from Colossians 1:27.

Dear God, you are infinite, eternal, and deeper than I can ever understand. Thank you for graciously revealing yourself to me in Jesus Christ by your Spirit. I marvel that my relationship with you will continually be full of discovery for the rest of my life. Please give me the assurance and knowledge of this mystery, which is Christ in me, the hope of eternal glory. In Jesus' name, amen.

EPHESIANS 2:4-5

But because of his great love for us, God, who is rich in mercy, made us alive with Christ even when we were dead in transgressions—it is by grace you have been saved.

GOD IS A TRINITY

May the grace of the Lord Jesus Christ, and the love of God, and the fellowship of the Holy Spirit be with you all. (2 Corinthians 13:14)

God is beyond our full understanding, and it's difficult to wrap our human minds around him. God the Father, God the Son (Jesus), and God the Holy Spirit are each fully God. Does that mean there are three gods? No. The Bible teaches that there is only one God. Does that mean that the Father, the Son, and the Spirit are the same? No. As Christians, we believe in one God in a way that doesn't deny the distinctions between the Father, the Son, and the Spirit. This is the mystery of the Trinity.

Together the Father, Son and Holy Spirit do all things. Nevertheless, the Father is generally connected with creation, making the world. The Son, Jesus, is generally connected to redemption, making us right with God. The Holy Spirit is generally connected with growing us to be more like God. The Holy Spirit helps us grow by giving us under-standing, by bringing our sin to our attention, so we can repent and be forgiven, and by guiding us to follow the Lord.

The Father sent Jesus to earth to be born, die, rise again, and ascend to heaven. Together the Father and Son sent the Spirit, who brings God's people into relationship with the Father and Son. "I will ask the Father, and he will give you another advocate to help you and be with you forever—the Spirit of truth. The world cannot accept him, because it neither sees him nor knows him. But you know him, for he lives with you and will be in you" (John 14:15–17). The Holy Spirit will give you courage, enable you to hear God's voice, and give you words to speak when you share Jesus with others.

READ

Answer these questions after reading Matthew 3:13–17 and Psalm 131.

1. How can we observe all three Persons of the Trinity in Matthew 3:16–17?
2. How is the psalmist able to find peace even though he doesn't understand everything?
3. What are some of the distinctions between God the Father, God the Son, and God the Holy Spirit?
4. How do we see the unity of God the Father and God the Son and God the Holy Spirit?

PRAY

Today's prayer comes from Romans 1:1–4.

Dear God, I praise you for being my loving Father who created me. I praise you, Jesus, for saving me and being in charge of my life. I praise you, Holy Spirit, for living in me and giving me new life. Thank you, God, for promising the gospel in your word and for appointing your Son with power through the Spirit of holiness. I praise you, Lord, mysterious Three-in-One—Father, Son, and Holy Spirit. In Jesus' name, amen.

SHILO TAYLOR

GOD IS THE ONLY GOD

"You are my witnesses," declares the Lord, *"and my servant whom I have chosen, so that you may know and believe me and understand that I am he. Before me no god was formed, nor will there be one after me. I, even I, am the* Lord, *and apart from me there is no savior."* (Isaiah 43:10–11)

Many people believe there are many ways to heaven, and the important thing is to be good. However, Jesus says, "I am the way and the truth and the life. No one comes to the Father except through me" (John 14:6). There is only one way to heaven, and that is through Jesus Christ. Our salvation doesn't depend on our identity, our behavior, or how we measure up to other people. We are saved only because Jesus rescued us by dying on the cross in our place and rising again, getting rid of our sin forever and giving us new life. The only way to heaven is to believe in him and accept his sacrifice.

God is the only one worthy of the number one spot in our lives. We may fill that spot with people we love, goals we have, good deeds, or material things, but only God can fill a spot designed for him. "For great is the LORD and most worthy of praise; he is to be feared above all gods, for all the gods of the nations are idols, but the LORD made the heavens. Splendor and majesty are before him; strength and glory are in his sanctuary" (Psalm 96:4-6).

If God is so powerful, then why does it sometimes seem like evil is winning in the world? God is sovereign; he is the ultimate ruler. "Dominion belongs to the LORD and he rules over the nations" (Psalm 22:28). This is true, even though sometimes it seems as if evil is winning in our world. God is in control even when everything looks broken and painful. Until Jesus returns to make everything right, we still live in a sinful and broken world. But he promises it won't be this way forever!

Jeremiah was a prophet who had seen the ugly in the world, but still knew who held the world. He said, "Ah, Sovereign LORD, you have made the heavens and the earth by your great power and outstretched arm. Nothing is too hard for you" (Jeremiah 32:17).

READ

Answer these questions after reading Isaiah 44:6-8 and Isaiah 45:5-7.

1. What do you think it means that God is the first and the last? (See Isaiah 44:6.)
2. What things—relationships, objects, goals—have you put in a place ahead of God?
3. How does God answer the question, "Is there any God besides me?" (See Isaiah 44:8.)
4. According to Isaiah 45:7, what are some of the things God is in control of in this life?

PRAY

Today's prayer comes from the Apostles' Creed:

> I believe in God the Father almighty, creator of heaven and earth. In Jesus' name, amen.

GOD IS EVERYWHERE AND GOD KNOWS EVERYTHING

"Am I only a God nearby," declares the LORD, *"and not a God far away? Who can hide in secret places so that I cannot see them?"* declares the LORD. *"Do not I fill heaven and earth?"* declares the LORD. (Jeremiah 23:23–24)

Have you ever hoped for a friend who would be there for you no matter what? A friend who knows everything about you, even anticipating what you'll say next? A friend who never leaves you lonely and who understands you even before you explain yourself?

God understands you, he knows everything about you (yes, even the embarrassing parts), and he is always there for you. "Where can I go from your Spirit?" the psalmist exclaims. "Where can I flee from your presence? If I go up to the heavens, you are there; if I make my bed in the depths, you are there" (Psalm 139:7–8).

You can't run away from God. Even your thoughts are known to him. "Before a word is on my tongue you, LORD, know it completely" (Psalm 139:4). The darkness will never be dark enough to hide you from him. "Even the darkness will not be dark to you; the night will shine like the day, for darkness is as light to you" (Psalm 139:12).

Nothing surprises God. He created you, and he knows you better than you know yourself! Think of a time in your life when you felt lonely or abandoned, or a time when you thought no one saw what you saw. God was there every time. God is everywhere. He cares for his people across the world, accomplishes his purposes in all places, and sees your hurts and dreams, all at the same time. He hears the prayers you pray. He even hears your prayers that you think don't make sense. Not only does he know, but he also cares.

READ

Answer these questions after reading Romans 8:26–39.

1. What verse from today meant the most to you? Why?
2. Have you ever tried to escape God?
   If so, what happened?
3. How does knowing that God sees all and knows
   all affect your relationship with him?
4. Is there a situation in your life that is frustrating or
   disappointing to you? If so, how does the truth of
   Romans 8:28 affect your perspective of that situation?

PRAY

Today's prayer comes from Hebrews 4:13 and Romans 8:39.

Father, you are everywhere, and you know everything.
Thank you that nothing is hidden from you. Thank you
for knowing everything and loving and pursuing me.
Thank you for always understanding me and always
being with me. Help me run to you, instead of away from
you. Nothing can separate us from your love that is in
Christ Jesus our Lord. In Jesus' name, amen.

GOD IS LOVE THAT WON'T FADE

In all these things we are more than conquerors through him who loved us. For I am convinced that neither death nor life, neither angels nor demons, neither the present nor the future, nor any powers, neither height nor depth, nor anything else in all creation, will be able to separate us from the love of God that is in Christ Jesus our Lord. (Romans 8:37–39)

All around us we see love fail. We see relationships end in breakups. We see marriages end in divorce. We see friendships end. Some love us based on our performance. They love us as long as we look good, keep it together, and do what they want. We love people who don't love us back or maybe they love us but do a lousy job showing it. We let people down and miss opportunities to love well. We think we love, but we doubt our love when our feelings go away and the relationship has challenges.

God's love is nothing like those "loves." His love endures forever. God's love is not based on what we do or don't do. Our choices bring consequences, and they must be faced, but they won't change God's love for us. God pursues us no matter how much we reject him. His love for us is unconditional and permanent. "You, Lord, are a compassionate and gracious God, slow to anger, abounding in love and faithfulness" (Psalm 86:15).

Jesus' death and resurrection are the grandest acts of love anyone will ever do for you. Jesus left his throne in heaven to come to earth as a humble person who was beaten and killed, a Savior who offered himself on a cross as your sacrifice. Clearly Jesus' love for you is not empty, mushy, or wimpy. It is strong and unfailing. His death and resurrection took away your sin and gives you true life with him. He can back up his promises to care for you and meet your needs.

The love of God changes who we are and how we relate to other people. His love is unfailingly patient, kind, protecting, merciful, and hopeful. His love seeps into us, and then it pours back out of us onto the people around us. His love gives us strength to do things that seem impossible.

READ

Answer these questions after reading 1 John 4:7–21.

1. What did you learn in this passage about God's love for you?

2. In what ways do you tend to respond to God's love?
3. How does God's love impact your life?
4. Why must Christians love each other? (See 1 Corinthians 13.)

PRAY

Today's prayer comes from Psalm 136:1 and Zephaniah 3:17.

> Lord, your love endures forever. Thank you for being the Mighty Warrior who saves us and delights in us. Teach me to rejoice because in your love you rejoice over us! Your love never fails. Help me accept your love and share it with others. In Jesus' name, amen.

DEUTERONOMY 6:4-5

Hear, O Israel: The Lord our God, the Lord is one. Love the Lord your God with all your heart and with all your soul and with all your strength.

GOD IS PERFECT AND UNCHANGING

He is the Rock, his works are perfect, and all his ways are just. A faithful God who does no wrong, upright and just is he. (Deuteronomy 32:4)

We've all been disappointed by someone important to us. We've all had our trust betrayed. We've all wondered at some point, "Is there anyone I can trust?" And even when we try hard, we let others down. All people sin. Be encouraged! God doesn't mess up. He's not weak. He doesn't back down. He never goes back on his word. You can always trust him—even when everything else fails.

We don't always understand what God is doing, but his plans are perfect and his timing is right. This doesn't mean our lives will always be easy. It doesn't mean we won't question why he is doing something. It doesn't mean we will always have all the answers we want. We may not understand or even agree with everything God does, but we can still know he is perfect and his ways are perfect. God is a promise keeper and will follow through: "Not one word has failed of all the good promises he gave through his servant Moses" (1 Kings 8:56).

We can be confident that God is perfect and unchanging. "Jesus Christ is the same yesterday and today and forever" (Hebrews 13:8). His character will never waver. His word is as true today as it was thousands of years ago. The world is broken, but he is not. The world changes and fails, but he is sure and solid. As the prophet Isaiah says, "All people are like grass, and all their faithfulness is like the flowers of the field. ... The grass withers and the flowers fall, but the word of our God endures forever" (Isaiah 40:6, 8).

READ

Answer these questions after reading Psalm 18.

1. What did you learn in this psalm about God's reliability?
2. When have you trusted God to be perfect and unchanging?
3. Why do you think this psalm compares God to a rock?
4. How does the psalmist respond to God's perfect, unchanging character?

PRAY

Today's prayer comes from Psalm 89:1–2, 8.

Lord, your love stands firm forever. I will sing of your great love forever; I will make your faithfulness known through all generations. O LORD God Almighty, who is like you? You are mighty, and your faithfulness surrounds you. In Jesus' name, amen.

GOD IS A REFUGE

You have been a refuge for the poor, a refuge for the needy in their distress, a shelter from the storm and a shade from the heat. For the breath of the ruthless is like a storm driving against a wall and like the heat of the desert. You silenced the uproar of foreigners; as heat is reduced by the shadow of a cloud, so the song of the ruthless is stilled. (Isaiah 25:4–5)

God is a refuge. He is a shelter, a safe place where we can rest even when things around us are terrifying. God not only understands our circumstances, but he also protects us when we are out of strength. While our lives may feel like they are spinning out of control, "Under his wings you will find refuge; his faithfulness will be your shield and rampart" (Psalm 91:4).

When you feel like no one understands you, when you're afraid, discouraged, anxious, or desperate, when you want to run away or harm yourself, pray with the psalmist, "Have mercy on me, my God, have mercy on me, for in you I take refuge. I will take refuge in the shadow of your wings until the disaster has passed" (Psalm 57:1).

We can bring our mess, our broken pieces, and our out-of-control life to God. He can put us together. We don't have to fix ourselves before we go to God. We rest—alone and with others—when we read the Bible, when we pour out our heart in prayer, when we talk about God's promises and great deeds. Our rest comes from God, our refuge.

God says, "Be still, and know that I am God; I will be exalted among the nations, I will be exalted in the earth" (Psalm 46:10). How can you be still and rest in God as your refuge today? Try turning off your phone, computer, or any distractions for a while. Find a way to be still. Go for a walk and let your mind be still or find a cozy spot to close your eyes and think about the verses you've read. Ask another Christian to tell you about a time God was their refuge. Be still and think about the words in a song or Bible reading during church. Take time to pray and rest so God can calm your fears. Be still and know that he is God.

READ

Answer these questions after reading Psalm 46.

1. What do you need strength to face today?
2. What fears or struggles do you need to trust God to be your refuge for?
3. How does knowing that God is your strength affect your view of difficult situations? (See Psalm 46:2–3.)

4. In what areas of your life do you need to "Be still, and know that [he] is God" (Psalm 46:10)?

PRAY

Today's prayer comes from Psalm 71:3-8.

> Dear Lord, you are my rock of refuge. Save me, for you are my rock and my fortress. Deliver me, O my God, from the hand of the wicked. I will praise and thank you, O sovereign LORD; you are my hope and my confidence. (Ask God for his strength in a specific situation in your life.) In Jesus' name, amen.

GOD IS THE ULTIMATE WARRIOR

The Lord is my strength and my defense; he has become my salvation. ... The Lord is a warrior; the Lord is his name. ... Your right hand, Lord, was majestic in power. Your right hand, Lord, shattered the enemy. (Exodus 15:2, 3, 6)

God is love. He is forgiving and merciful. This doesn't mean God is a pushover. God is also a warrior. He is just, strong, and uncompromising. He has no equal. Yet our ideas of strength don't totally apply here. God came to earth in weakness as baby. He who governs the universe was sentenced to death by a human governor. He defeated death through his cross and resurrection. "[Jesus] too shared in [our] humanity so that by his death he might break the power of him who holds the power of death—that is, the devil—and free those who all their lives were held in slavery by their fear of death" (Hebrews 2:14–15).

The Lord fights for us and through us. We are involved with him in a very real spiritual battle. We can't stay neutral. "Be alert and of sober mind. Your enemy the devil prowls around like a roaring lion looking for someone to devour. Resist him, standing firm in the faith, because you know that the family of believers throughout the world is undergoing the same kind of sufferings" (1 Peter 5:8–9).

Don't be fooled. Your power, strength, and fame aren't powerful. You can't defeat the enemy (Satan) on your own. Acknowledge your weakness and lack of control. "Cast all your anxiety on God because he cares for you. ... And the God of all grace, who called you to his eternal glory in Christ, after you have suffered a little while, will himself restore you and make you strong, firm, and steadfast" (1 Peter 5:7, 10).

If you follow Jesus, you are on the side that wins (read Revelation 20:7–15 for a glimpse into that future battle). As with any battle, fighting a spiritual battle takes time and training to fight. You don't sit on the couch eating junk food or numb your brain with social media to prepare for a physical battle. You work with a trainer—in a spiritual battle, this is a small group leader, pastor, church members. You master your weapons—your spiritual weapons are the Bible and prayer. You orient your life—work, meals, and rest—around this preparation. You don't get to sit this one out.

READ

Answer these questions after reading Ephesians 6:10–20.

1. Compare and contrast spiritual armor with military armor.
2. How should you prepare for spiritual battles in your life?
3. Who is the enemy that you are fighting in these spiritual battles? (See Ephesians 6:12.)
4. What changes do you need to make in your life in order to to "be alert and always keep on praying for the Lord's people" (Ephesians 6:28)?

PRAY

Today's prayer comes from Deuteronomy 31:6.

> Dear Lord, you reign forever and ever. Only by your strength and Spirit can I be prepared for the battles before me. Help me to be strong and courageous and not to be afraid. You are the Lord God who goes with me and you will never leave nor forsake me. In Jesus' name, amen.

GOD IS FORGIVENESS

If we confess our sins, he is faithful and just and will forgive us our sins and purify us from all unrighteousness. (1 John 1:9)

Have you ever felt guilty for something you've done or thought? Have you wondered if God could really forgive and change you?

No matter how hard we try, we all have a sin problem. "All have sinned and fall short of the glory of God" (Romans 3:23). God also knows our sin problem and has redeemed us in Christ! "And all are justified freely by his grace through the redemption that came by Christ Jesus" (Romans 3:24).

We all need forgiveness, and we all suffer guilt—sometimes even after we've received forgiveness. David is a great biblical example of this truth. He needed serious forgiveness. He was a king of Israel who loved God, but he messed up and kept messing up. He lusted after a married woman, Bathsheba. After he took advantage of her, he had her husband killed to cover his tracks.

When David sinned, God sent a prophet to confront him. "You are the man! ... Why did you despise the word of the LORD by doing what is evil in his eyes?" (2 Samuel 12:7, 9). David realized he was making himself miserable. He acknowledged and confessed his sin. He still faced consequences for his sin, and he couldn't undo the wrongs he committed. However, he was mercifully reconciled to God. Even amid his consequences, David worshiped God, assured that God had put away his sin.

In Psalm 51 we read David's confession of these sins. He first acknowledges God's character and his own sin. He then asks to be cleansed of his guilt. He asks God to change him and replace his heavy, shame-filled heart with the joy of God's salvation. He promises to tell what God has done for him and to worship God.

READ

Answer these questions after reading Psalm 51.

1. How did David respond when God exposed his sin? (See 2 Samuel 12:13.)

2. How do you tend to respond when God exposes your sin?

3. Even though David's sin affected several people, who does he say he sinned against in Psalm 51:4? Why is that significant?

4. If the Lord is revealing sin in your life today, use David's model of repentance: acknowledge God's

just and forgiving character and your sin, ask for
forgiveness, ask God to change you, and thank him.

PRAY

Today's prayer comes from Psalm 139:23 and Psalm 51:10–12.

Lord, you are holy. Search me, and know my heart; test
me and know my thoughts. Reveal to me any overlooked
sin in my life. I am sinful and unclean. Create in me a
pure heart, O God, and renew a right spirit within me.
Do not cast me from your presence or take your Holy
Spirit from me. Restore to me the joy of your salvation
and grant me a willing spirit, to sustain me. In Jesus'
name, amen.

2 TIMOTHY 3:16-17

All Scripture is God-breathed and is useful for teaching, rebuking, correcting and training in righteousness, so that the servant of God may be thoroughly equipped for every good work.

DAY TWENTY-NINE

GOD IS PERSONAL

Your hands made me and formed me. (Psalm 119:73)

The Lord didn't just create us and let things go without getting involved. God created the heavens and earth, plant and animal life, and he made us with intricate detail and uniqueness. God puts great care into all the things he makes. With loving purpose he designed your physical appearance, your mind, your talents, and your personality. He delights in what he has made and longs to know you.

God has always dwelled with his people. In the garden of Eden he dwelled with Adam and Eve. After Adam and Eve sinned, God went to extravagant lengths to pursue his people. He sent prophets with his message, and he gave the Israelites instructions for the tabernacle, where his presence would be. Then Jesus came to earth. After the ascension, God poured the Holy Spirit into our hearts so that God will always be present with us. He will never leave or forsake us.

If you struggle with your identity, if you are insecure about the way God made you, if you tend to criticize yourself, then take extra time reading through today's psalm. Notice how God through the psalmist defines your identity. Observe how the psalmist describes how God made you. Write down the verses that stick out to you. Post them so you can be reminded of God's love for you. You are not an accident. His hands made you and formed you. God values you and is thrilled about your life. He gladly dwells with you!

READ

Answer these questions after reading Psalm 139.

1. How does Psalm 139 change the way you see yourself?
2. What are some unique things about you?
3. According to Psalm 139:1–5, how well does God know you? How does that reality make you feel?
4. How does it impact your view of your perceived flaws to know that you are "fearfully and wonderfully made" (Psalm 139:14)?

PRAY

Today's prayer comes from Psalm 139.

> Father, you knit me together in my mother's womb. Thank you for making me the way you did. Help me to see myself as you see me: as your beloved child in whom you are well pleased. Thank you that I have value because I am yours! In Jesus' name, amen.

PART THREE

LIVING LIFE
WITH GOD

CHURCH—A BUILDING CAN'T CONTAIN IT

God has put the body together, giving greater honor to the parts that lacked it, so that there should be no division in the body, but that its parts should have equal concern for each other. If one part suffers, every part suffers with it; if one part is honored, every part rejoices with it. Now you are the body of Christ, and each one of you is a part of it. (1 Corinthians 12:24–27)

The church is made up of people who believe Jesus is their Savior and have made him first in their lives. The church isn't made up of perfect people. It is made of people who are learning about following Christ and learning how to love God and each other.

The church, which includes all Christ-followers, meets regularly all across the globe in smaller organizations known as local churches. A local church can meet in a small building, a home, or a stadium, but a church isn't the building itself. The church is made up of people who are following Jesus. No matter how young you are when you became a Christian, there is a place for you to be part of a local church! It's important to find a place in your community where you can learn and serve.

The church doesn't gather to be entertained. God's desire is for the church to encourage each other, pray together, and learn together. We get to worship together, hear God's word, and serve others. We get to discover and enjoy the gifts God gives us! The church gathers to experience God's grace together in Christ.

In Acts we read that the church "devoted themselves to the apostles' teaching and to fellowship, to the breaking of bread and to prayer" (Acts 2:42). This common life involved more than meeting in a building once a week and then going their separate ways. They ate together. They prayed together. They gave what they had to help the needy and the hurting. They shared—through their words and actions—the good news that Jesus promises forgiveness and life to those who believe in him. Through the church God works in the world.

READ

Answer these questions after reading Acts 2:37–47.

1. What comes to mind when you think of a "church"?
2. What did you learn about God's plan for the church in Acts 2?
3. Why is it important for you to be part of a local church?

4. If you are part of a local church, in what ways is your church similar to the church in Acts 2? How is it different?

PRAY

Today's prayer comes from the Apostles' Creed.

> I believe in the Holy Spirit, the holy Christian* church, the communion of saints, the forgiveness of sins, the resurrection of the body, and the life everlasting. In Jesus' name, amen.

*Some churches say "the holy catholic church," which means the universal church—the church across all time and space. When uncapitalized the word "catholic" simply means "universal." To avoid confusion I've used "the holy Christian church" instead.

BAPTISM—IT'S NOT JUST WATER

Don't you know that all of us who were baptized into Christ Jesus were baptized into his death? We were therefore buried with him through baptism into death in order that, just as Christ was raised from the dead through the glory of the Father, we too may live a new life. (Romans 6:3–4)

Jesus tells us to baptize: "Go and make disciples of all nations, baptizing them in the name of the Father and of the Son and of the Holy Spirit" (Matthew 28:19). Some Christians sprinkle water and some dunk in a pool, river, or lake; in each of these ways the church obeys Jesus' command.

Jesus removes your sin and transforms you. Baptism illustrates our salvation in Jesus. In baptism we are identified with Jesus' death, burial, and resurrection. As the water washes over us, we realize our old, broken, sinful self has been put to death and raised to new life. "If we have been united with him in a death like his, we will certainly be united with him in a resurrection like his. For we know that our old self was crucified with him so that the body ruled by sin might be done away with, that we should no longer be slaves to sin—because anyone who has died has been set free from sin" (Romans 6:5–7). Jesus forgives us and gives us new life with him.

Baptism reminds us of our new life with God. Baptism reminds us that we haven't fixed ourselves; Jesus has forgiven us and washed us clean by his grace. We are not our own. In baptism God seals what he has done in making you new. Your church celebrates your faith with you!

READ

Answer these questions after reading Matthew 3 and Colossians 2:9–3:17.

1. What new thing did you learn about baptism?
2. What is baptism a picture of? (See Colossians 2:12.)
3. Have you been baptized? If so, describe that experience.
4. If you have committed your life to Jesus but you haven't been baptized, talk to your pastor or small group leader about it.

PRAY

Today's prayer comes from Romans 6:3-4.

> Lord, thank you for baptism. Having been baptized into
> Jesus' death and resurrection, may we put away our old
> life of sin. Renew our minds and guide us by your Holy
> Spirit that we may live in holiness. In Jesus' name, amen.

COMMUNION—IT'S NOT A SNACK

Jesus said to them, "Very truly I tell you, unless you eat the flesh of the Son of Man and drink his blood, you have no life in you. Whoever eats my flesh and drinks my blood has eternal life, and I will raise them up at the last day. (John 6:53–54)

The night Jesus was betrayed, he celebrated the Passover with his disciples. Every year the Israelites celebrate Passover to remember when God miraculously rescued them from Egypt by protecting them with lamb's blood on their doorposts and nourishing them with lamb meat. Jesus revealed that there is more to the Passover they had always celebrated. Passover pointed to what he did on the cross. His blood covers and protects us, saving us from death! His body was given for us; he will sustain and nourish us during our life's journey.

Jesus offered himself so that we have life and forgiveness. We remember and celebrate this reality when we take Communion—what some churches call the Lord's Supper or the Eucharist. Believers drink wine or juice and eat bread together. In this meal we refocus on our relationship with Jesus and one another.

In Communion we remember Jesus' sacrifice on the cross for us. "The Lord Jesus ... took bread, and when he had given thanks, he broke it and said, 'This is my body, which is for you; do this in remembrance of me.' In the same way, after supper he took the cup, saying, 'This cup is the new covenant in my blood; do this, whenever you drink it, in remembrance of me'" (1 Corinthians 11:23–25).

In Communion we slow down to examine ourselves. "Everyone ought to examine themselves before they eat of the bread and drink from the cup" (1 Corinthians 11:28). We confess our sins, we ask God to forgive us, and we reconcile with one another.

In Communion we declare that Jesus is coming back. "Whenever you eat this bread and drink this cup, you proclaim the Lord's death until he comes" (1 Corinthians 11:26).

In Communion we bring our sin, fear, and weakness to Jesus. And he blots out our sin, comforts us, and strengthens us. "Taste and see that the Lord is good; blessed is the one who takes refuge in him" (Psalm 34:8).

READ

Answer these questions after reading Matthew 26:26–30.

1. What did you learn about Communion today?
2. Why do you think Communion is important?
3. In what ways is Communion similar to the Passover meal?
4. Why do you think it is important for us to examine ourselves before we take Communion?

PRAY

Today's prayer comes from 1 Corinthians 10:16–17.

Jesus, you feed us with the spiritual food of your body and blood. Thank you for offering yourself as the sacrifice for our sin. May we receive it thankfully in remembrance of you. The bread we break and the cup of thanksgiving are participation in your body and blood. By your Spirit give me and all those who are in your church the strength and courage to love and serve you. In your name, amen.

PSALM 139:7-8

Where can I go from your Spirit? Where can I flee from your presence? If I go up to the heavens, you are there; if I make my bed in the depths, you are there.

WORSHIP—MORE THAN SINGING

Come, let us bow down in worship, let us kneel before the LORD our Maker; for he is our God and we are the people of his pasture, the flock under his care. (Psalm 95:6–7)

Worship is all about who God is. By worship we honor God and submit to him. True worship makes God our highest priority and acknowledge our life comes from him. "Sing to the LORD, all the earth; proclaim his salvation day after day. Declare his glory among the nations, his marvelous deeds among all peoples. For great is the LORD and most worthy of praise; he is to be feared above all gods" (1 Chronicles 16:23–25).

We are privileged to worship God. When we declare in thought, word, or action that Jesus is Lord of our lives, we are worshiping. Worship is saying who God is and what he has done. Who he is and what he has done lead us to confess and repent our sins, to hear and respond to his word, to sing his praises, and to take Communion. These acts of worship aren't restricted to a Sunday church service!

In worship we spend time with God, whether we're happy or sad. We can and should spend time with God in the various phases of our lives. In rough times we can cry out to him and confide in him. In awesome moments we can celebrate and rejoice with him. In every up and down we can praise him and talk with him. No circumstance can prevent us from worshiping God.

Christians worship God by ourselves and with others. We can sing at the top of our lungs in our car and we can worship with our church on Sunday. We can lie silently under the stars and we can listen quietly to others. We can read the Bible with our family after dinner, with our friends after school, and by ourselves in the morning.

Worship can be painting and writing, hiking and relaxing. We can even worship God by helping with chores and volunteering our time. Worship is praying, giving, serving, and sharing life.

God created you uniquely. He wants you to praise him in a way that celebrates your relationship with him. He created you to worship with other Christians too. Your faith is not meant to be lived alone!

READ

Answer these questions after reading Psalm 84.

1. In what ways does your life show you worship God?
2. What do you think of when you hear the word "worship"?
3. Have you ever had a strong desire to praise and worship God? (See Psalm 84:1–2.) If so, describe that experience.
4. Ask God how he wants you to worship him today.

PRAY

Today's prayer comes from the Apostles' Creed.

I believe in God the Father almighty, creator of heaven and earth. I believe in Jesus Christ, his only Son, our Lord. He was conceived by the Holy Spirit and born of the Virgin Mary. He suffered under Pontius Pilate, was crucified, died, and was buried. He descended to the dead. On the third day he rose again from the dead. He ascended into heaven. He is seated at the right hand of the Father. He will come to judge the living and the dead. I believe in the Holy Spirit, the holy Christian* church, the communion of saints, the forgiveness of sins, the resurrection of the body, and the life everlasting. In Jesus' name, amen.

*Some churches say "the holy catholic church," which means the universal church—the church across all time and space. When uncapitalized the word "catholic" simply means "universal." To avoid confusion I've used "the holy Christian church" instead.

PRAYER — TALKING WITH GOD

Lord, teach us to pray. (Luke 11:1)

Prayer can be intimidating. Praying in front of people can be even more intimidating. Fortunately, God doesn't require fancy words or long prayers. He wants what every close friend wants: open, honest, frequent conversations. That involves talking and listening.

Even though God knows everything about you and everything you need, he wants to hear your thoughts and requests. But prayer is more than just asking God for things. If you only list what you want God to do for you, you will quickly grow frustrated. God wants to speak with you and to grow his relationship with you. And like in any relationship, this requires regular practice and attention. Prayer will line up your ideas with God's. "Your will be done, on earth as it is in heaven" (Matthew 6:10).

In the Gospel of Luke, Jesus models this for us. For example, knowing that he will soon be arrested, tried, and executed, he prepares by praying in a quiet garden. He prays earnestly, pouring out his heart and wrestling in prayer. He asks for the strength to submit to God's will. "Father, if you are willing, take this cup from me; yet not my will, but yours be done" (Luke 22:42).

Psalm 31 is another example of prayer. David describes God as his refuge and only help. He tells God his fears, problems, and discouragement. As he prays, he remembers God's strength and unfailing love. He ends his prayer praising God, confident he can do anything in the Lord's strength!

Let God do this with you. Begin your prayer by acknowledging something about God. Then pour out your fears and your thoughts. Listen to him in prayer and in Scripture; let him remind you of his character and actions. Close your prayers with praise. By the end of your prayers he might give you a new perspective or an idea of how to deal with something. God longs to transform you into the image of Jesus and to give you comfort and peace.

READ

Answer these questions after reading Psalm 31.

1. What words or phrases stood out to you as you read David pouring out his concerns to God?

2. What phrases does David use to acknowledge who God is?

3. When David called to God for help (Psalm 31:22), how did God respond?

4. Today find a prayer spot—a quiet place, free of distraction, where you can focus on God as you pray.

PRAY

Today's prayer is the prayer Jesus taught his disciples (Luke 11:1–4; Matthew 6:9–13). It's known as the Lord's Prayer:

> Our Father in heaven, hallowed be your name, your kingdom come, your will be done, on earth as it is in heaven. Give us this day our daily bread. And forgive us our debts, as we also have forgiven our debtors. And lead us not into temptation, but deliver us from the evil one. For the kingdom, the power, and the glory are yours now and forever. Amen.

GIVING—WHAT WE DO WITH WHAT WE HAVE

Where your treasure is, there your heart will be also.
(Matthew 6:21)

In the Old Testament God commanded the Israelites to give their firstfruits—their best—to him. They brought 10 percent of their money for the priests (called a tithe—meaning, a "tenth"). They gave to God the best and first of their animals, their land, and their crops. These tithes and offerings reminded them that all that they have they have received from God. God had given them their abilities, their land, and their harvest. They could easily begin thinking that a successful harvest was a result of their intelligence, their hard work, and their good ideas. But it was all God's blessing!

Tithing requires an attitude of thankfulness and generosity. The act of giving can't be separated from the attitude of giving. "'The multitude of your sacrifices—what are they to me?' says the LORD. 'I have more than enough of burnt offerings, of rams and the fat of fattened animals; I have no pleasure in the blood of bulls and lambs and goats. ... Stop bringing meaningless offerings!'" (Isaiah 1:11, 13). We can't just go through the motions of giving. "For I desire mercy, not sacrifice, and acknowledgment of God rather than burnt offerings" (Hosea 6:6). God desires our hearts, not only our stuff.

Jesus reminds us why God commanded tithes and offerings in the first place: to honor God and to acknowledge his blessings. Jesus teaches that the amount of money isn't important; rather, it's about acknowledging that all things come from God. We should use everything he has given us to honor him and bless others. "Each of you should give what you have decided in your heart to give, not reluctantly or under compulsion, for God loves a cheerful giver" (2 Corinthians 9:7). We should say, "Wow, God, everything comes from you, so how can I use everything to honor you?"

READ

Answer these questions after reading Mark 12:38–44.

1. Why did Jesus warn against the teachers of the law?
2. How much did the widow give to God?
3. Why was the widow's gift considered more than all the others? (See Mark 12:43–44.)
4. What are some specific ways that you can dedicate your time, talents, and possessions to the Lord? Commit now to what you will give him.

PRAY

Today's prayer comes from 2 Corinthians 9:7.

> Lord, everything comes from you. Thank you. I want to honor you with all you've given me. Help me see how I can bless others with what you've given me. By your power, make me a cheerful giver! In Jesus' name, amen.

SERVICE—BEING ABOUT MORE THAN YOURSELF

Do nothing out of selfish ambition or vain conceit. Rather, in humility value others above yourselves, not looking to your own interests but each of you to the interests of the others. (Philippians 2:3-4)

Jesus washed his disciples' feet as an act of service. Jesus, our God and King, chose to wash his disciples' nasty, dirty, calloused feet that probably didn't have nicely clipped toenails. This humiliating task was reserved for lowly servants. The disciples were appalled. Yet Jesus persisted. He showed love and a servant's heart. He defined what Christian leadership is. "Now that I, your Lord and Teacher, have washed your feet, you also should wash one another's feet. I have set an example that you should do as I have done for you" (John 13:14-15).

Serving isn't just for people who like to clean up messes. It is for everyone. God asks that we go out of our way to help others, meet others' needs, and put others first. Our natural self-centeredness makes it painful and difficult to serve others—especially people we don't like. We want to look good. We want to get something in return for our kindness. Yet nothing should take priority over loving God and loving people.

"In your relationships with one another, have the same mindset as Christ Jesus: Who, being in very nature God, did not consider equality with God something to be used to his own advantage; rather, he made himself nothing by taking the very nature of a servant, being made in human likeness. And being found in appearance as a man, he humbled himself by becoming obedient to death—even death on a cross!" (Philippians 2:5–8).

READ

Answer these questions after reading John 13:1–17.

1. When have other people gone out of their way to serve you? Describe the circumstances.
2. Why do you think Jesus says, "You also should wash one another's feet" (John 13:14)?
3. Why is service to others important?
4. Who can you serve today? How?

PRAY

Today's prayer comes from Mark 10:45.

> Jesus, you came not to be served, but to serve and to give your life as a ransom for us. Teach me to follow your example in serving others. In your name, amen.

2 CORINTHIANS 12:9

My grace is sufficient for you, for my power is made perfect in weakness.

FELLOWSHIP—TAKING FRIENDSHIP UP A NOTCH

As iron sharpens iron, so one person sharpens another.
(Proverbs 27:17)

Christians spend time together to grow in their walk with God and encourage each other. Christians call this "fellowship." God created us to have healthy relationships with each other, not to face things alone.

That's why God made the church, also called the body of Christ (read 1 Corinthians 12:12–31). We work better together and stay stronger together. We remind each other to have faith when life is confusing and it's hard to keep going. We share what we are learning to help each other. As the body is made up of many members, so also is the church. We don't all have the same abilities and gifts. Each of us uniquely contributes to the body of Christ. "If the ear should say, 'Because I am not an eye, I do not belong to the body,' it would not for that reason stop being part of the body. If the whole body were an eye, where would the sense of hearing be?" (1 Corinthians 12:16–17). We need each other. We should be excited about others' abilities and gifts—especially when they differ from our own. We shouldn't be jealous, wishing to be different than we are. "In fact God has placed the parts in the body, every one of them, just as he wanted them to be. If they were all one part, where would the body be?" (1 Corinthians 12:18–19). For example, God made some of us to teach, some of us to organize, some of us to lead music, and some to build up. We can't grow in our Christian faith all alone. You need others, and others need you! Each person has a part to play!

We need to build friendships with non-Christians. But we also need Christian friends to strengthen our faith, challenge us, build us up, pray with us, struggle with us, and worship God with us. We need friends to confront us and tell us the gospel.

Think about the friends you have right now. How do they encourage you and teach you about God? How do they challenge you in your faith and help you grow stronger? How can you pray with them and for them?

Seek fellowship with friends from school, family, a church small group, a mentor, a pastor. In the body of Christ you are able to share your struggles, to pray together, and to learn about God together.

"You are the body of Christ, and each one of you is a part of it" (1 Corinthians 12:27). We can't live the Christian life on our own—thank God that we aren't meant to!

READ

Answer these questions after reading Luke 5:17–26.

1. What did you learn in Luke 5:17–26 about the power of friendship?
2. Why is fellowship important?
3. Who in your life can you have fellowship with?
4. How can you build relationships with other Christians?

PRAY

Today's prayer comes from 1 Corinthians 12:25–27.

> Lord, there should be no division among your people. We should care for one another. If one of us suffers, we all suffer with that person; if one of us is honored, we all rejoice with that person. Help me grow in fellowship with your people. Give me wisdom to build godly friendships for mutual encouragement. In Jesus' name, amen.

EVANGELISM—IT'S FOR EVERYONE

Go and make disciples of all nations, baptizing them in the name of the Father and of the Son and of the Holy Spirit, and teaching them to obey everything I have commanded you. And surely I am with you always, to the very end of the age. (Matthew 28:19-20)

Evangelism is sharing the good news about Jesus forgiving our sins and giving us eternal life. Evangelism isn't just for pastors. God says all his people get to do this important job!

Before you break out in a sweat, worrying about how to talk about Jesus with someone, be assured that God is the one who saves. You don't save or give someone eternal life! God has given you an awesome role to play in what he is doing. You get to share about him, but he is the one who saves. The Holy Spirit will change hearts, just like he changed your heart when you became a Christian. You share the good news about Jesus, but the results are up to God. "Neither the one who plants nor the one who

waters is anything, but only God, who makes things grow"
(1 Corinthians 3:7).

You can evangelize as you share your own story, study
the Bible with others, or eat a meal with friends. God uses
every story. You might think your story is boring, but God's
faithfulness is never boring. Other people need to hear about
your faith and about God's faithfulness.

Before the crucifixion Peter was terrified of people find-
ing out he was a follower of Jesus. He denied even knowing
Christ. Jesus is faithful. He didn't give up on Peter when
Peter was weak. He reestablished Peter as a leader. Peter
didn't stay scared and quiet. By God's grace his past failures
didn't define him. The Holy Spirit gave him incredible courage to preach about Jesus and shepherd the church. (To find
out more, read the book of Acts!)

God has given you his Holy Spirit too. He is going to use
you in his amazing story. It's a story of turning the broken
and ugly into the perfect and complete. God our Redeemer
is the author of the best story ever, and we have a part to
play in it!

READ

Answer these questions after reading Acts 2:14–41

1. What does a "witness" do in a court trial?
   What does a "witness" talk about?

2. What do you think it means to be a "witness" for
   Jesus? What kinds of things would you talk about?

3. Who you can share the gospel with?
4. Pray for that person and ask the Lord to give you an opportunity to share with that person.

PRAY

Today's prayer comes from Colossians 4:3-6.

> Lord, you are the God who saves. Help me to clearly explain the gospel and to wisely make use of every opportunity. May my speech be gracious, so that I may know how to answer every person. In Jesus' name, amen.

A WORK IN PROGRESS

"Come, follow me," Jesus said, "and I will send you out to fish for people." At once they left their nets and followed him. (Mark 1:17–18)

Jesus comes to us. He calls us to follow him.

The choice that Adam and Eve made to disobey God, we make in our own ways again and again. We choose to sin, to place ourselves above God. But God chooses us in Jesus Christ. Jesus takes his holiness and puts it over us, covering our sin and shame so that we can have life with him. "Because of his great love for us, God, who is rich in mercy, made us alive with Christ even when we were dead in transgressions— it is by grace you have been saved" (Ephesians 2:4–5).

When we start to follow Jesus, we don't instantly live a perfect life. We don't return to the garden of Eden. In this world we still struggle and battle with sin. But the Lord doesn't leave us on our own to deal with sin and death. "My grace is sufficient for you, for my power is made perfect in weakness" (2 Corinthians 12:9). He grows us, changes us, and gives us purpose.

Right now we are a work in progress—and it's an important process! "And we all ... are being transformed into his image with ever-increasing glory, which comes from the Lord, who is the Spirit" (2 Corinthians 3:18). Our eternity is secure with God.

READ

Answer these questions after reading Ephesians 1:3–14.

1. According to Ephesians 1:4, when did God choose you? For what purpose did he choose you?

2. How does God seal his promise to you? (See Ephesians 1:13–14.)

3. Why is Jesus trustworthy? What did you learn about Jesus today?

4. Ask God to give you "the Spirit and wisdom and revelation, so that you may know him better" (Ephesians 1:17).

PRAY

Today's prayer comes from Romans 8:28–30.

Heavenly Father, you have chosen us in your Son, Jesus Christ. Thank you for choosing me, calling me, justifying me, and glorifying me. Teach me to trust that you work all things for the good of your people. Conform me to the image of Jesus. In Jesus' name, amen.

WHERE DO I GO FROM HERE?

Suppose one of you has a hundred sheep and loses one of them. Doesn't he leave the ninety-nine in the open country and go after the lost sheep until he finds it? And when he finds it, he joyfully puts it on his shoulders and goes home. Then he calls his friends and neighbors together and says, "Rejoice with me; I have found my lost sheep." I tell you that in the same way there will be more rejoicing in heaven over one sinner who repents than over ninety-nine righteous persons who do not need to repent. (Luke 15:4–7)

God pursues you like a shepherd searching for his lost sheep! He will not settle until he has found you. And then he will celebrate reestablishing a relationship with you.

Think about the person you feel the closest to. Think about the time and effort that goes into that relationship. Relationships can grow and strengthen or fade and break. To grow relationships requires quality time, openness, and encouragement. All the sacrifice and effort are worth it when you can know each other's thoughts just by a glance. It's worth it to have memories and fun things to look forward to together. It's worth it to be able to be unguarded about your thoughts and struggles. It's worth it when you realize the other person's good qualities are affecting and changing you.

Your relationship with the Lord also requires quality time and dedication. And it's more than worth it!

You have now spent forty days getting to know God better, asking hard questions, praying, and studying the Bible! Now you have the opportunity to decide what's next. Like all relationships, you can choose whether to keep investing time and effort in your relationship with God or not.

God isn't a friend who might not call back. He won't abandon you. He is your good shepherd, who leads and protects you. He has laid down his life for you. Learn to recognize his voice. These forty days are just the beginning of a life with God!

READ

Answer these questions after reading Psalm 63.

1. In what ways can you relate to the psalmist's desire to seek God and praise him?
2. Reflect on the past forty days. How has your faith changed? How has your life changed?
3. How will you seek God this week?

4. What will you do to continue to grow in your
    relationship with God? Ideas: Talk to your pastor
    or small group leader about books or studies
    you can do. Pick a prayer partner. Decide to
    memorize a verse every week. Choose a time
    during the day to have time with the Lord.

PRAY

Today's prayer is from Psalm 27:1, 7–11.

> Lord, you are my light and my salvation. Hear me when
> I call; be merciful to me and answer me! Thank you for
> growing me in this way: _____. Please give me
> direction and wisdom as I seek you. Surround me with
> people who will challenge me and help me grow. Your
> face, LORD, I will seek. Do not hide your face from me.
> Teach me your way, LORD. In Jesus' name, amen.